The Life and Times of . . .
A Very Special Boy
By
Noah Adams

(With a wee bit of help from Uncle Nigel and "Grumpy" Dadda Adams)

About Walter

Hi, my name is Walter George Thomas Abbot. But that's too hard to remember, so people just call me Walter. I'm aged 8 ¾, and this book is about some of the adventures I've had.

I'm from Northern Ireland, where I live with my Mammy, Sandra; my Daddy, Daniel; and my wee sister, Abigail, who is aged 6.

I should tell you from the start, that I'm kind of special. Special in two ways, actually.

First, I'm autistic (Asperger's Syndrome, they call my type of autism). The autism became apparent – at least to my parents - very early on in my life.

And here's how.

One day, when I was about 12-months-old, lying in my baby basket, just staring up at the ceiling, minding my own business, I suddenly felt a bit hungry.

"Excuse me," I called out, "Would somebody mind making me a nice bottle of warm milk, please. Thank you."

Well, my Mammy let out such a yelp, it nearly frightened the life out of me. Daddy just gasped, and whispered, loudly, "Who said that?"

"I said it." I called out to him, "Who did you think it was, somebody on the TV? Oh, and can one of you change my nappy, please. I've just had a wee accident."

It turned out they were shocked that somebody as young as me was able to talk so well. But they soon got used to it.

I've always loved words. As you can guess, I've been very, very good at them for as long as I can remember. So, it won't surprise you that books are one of my favourite things in the world. Another one is playing games on my tablet.

But I'm jumping ahead with the story.

Another shock for my parents came about a month after I spoke my first words to them.

One day, Mammy came home from shopping carrying a strange-looking, round thing with lots of wheels on it.

Me and daddy were relaxing at the time. I was lying on the settee watching University Challenge, and Daddy was sitting in his chair reading a book.

"Oh, I see that you got one," said Daddy to Mammy. Then, nodding in my direction, "That'll be great for the wee man."

"Excuse me, but what is this thing that'll be great for me?", I asked.

"It's called a walkie, love," Mammy replied, "It's to help you learn to walk when the time comes."
"But I don't need it. I can already walk," I told them.
"No, you can't, love," said Mammy laughing.

So, I got down from the settee and walked over to this round thing, looked at it for a second, turned it around for a bit, and said, "No thanks Mammy, as you can see, I don't really need it."

Mammy and Daddy were silent for a long while. Then Daddy asked me why I had never told them I could already walk.
"Because I'm faster at crawling," I told him, "And anyway, I like being carried." Then I giggled, "And I didn't want to shock you again."

There was another silence.

Eventually, Daddy pinched his arm a couple of times for some reason, then sighed and said, "Okay, I'll put it in the attic, and it'll do the next one."

To be honest, a few years later, when I watched my wee sister, Abagail, having fun, spinning around in it, I was sorry I hadn't made use of the walkie myself.

A wee bit more on the Asperger's later. But not too much. For autism isn't the most important reason that I'm special. Oh no, it certainly isn't. Not by a long way.

I also have Special Powers, you see. And there'll be an awful lot more about them in this book, as they're the main reason I have so many adventures.

I really hope that you enjoy reading about my adventures.

Lots of love,
Walter

Chapter 1

For a long time, I didn't realise I had Special Powers. I kind of discovered them by accident.

One day, I was in the playpark with Mammy and Abigail. I was sitting alone on the swings, when I noticed an older boy bullying a kid much younger than himself. Now, if there's one thing I can't stand, it's bullying. Well, there are lots of things I can't stand, actually, but I'll explain them as we go along.

The bully and the young kid were on the other side of the playpark from me and hadn't noticed that I was there. Suddenly, I found myself pointing across at them, and saying out loud in an angry voice, "Stop that, right now."

The bully stopped immediately, said sorry to the little kid, and put his arms around him. Then they started playing happily together.

I was so surprised; I nearly fell off my seat.
That must have been just a coincidence, I thought. But I decided to test it again, anyway.

Later that evening, Daddy was busy working in the garden. Without him noticing, I pointed at him and whispered, "Daddy, go to the shop and buy me some sweets." Nothing happened. He just carried on trimming our hedge. So, I thought, the bully incident had, after all, been just a coincidence. But actually, it wasn't.

A few weeks later, I was at home, sitting looking out of the front window, when I saw a man across the street with a big stick. He was dragging his poor dog along on a lead.

The dog didn't want to walk because it had a sore leg, but he was dragging it along anyway. He was nearly choking the poor thing. Again, without thinking, I pointed at him and shouted, "Stop that, right now."
And he did.

He stopped right away, started patting and stroking his dog, and then lifted it into his arms and walked away, hugging the wee pet as he went along.

After a few more experiments like this, I realised something very, very important about my special powers.

I can't use them for tiny, unimportant things, just to help myself. And certainly not for BAD THINGS.

They can only be used for GOOD THINGS. Mostly to help other people, and animals, that are being treated badly or unfairly.

I can of course use them to help myself if I'M being treated badly or unfairly, and most especially if I'm in danger - but just not for silly things.

I think my Special Powers are only there to help me try to make our world a better place, for all living things. And that includes plants, trees, and everything that lives in our oceans. It even includes aliens – as long as they're the friendly sort, of course.

(I really love the thought of meeting with friendly aliens someday. It would be wonderful, as long as we humans were just as friendly as the aliens.))

I decided early on that, in my mind, I would separate my special powers character from the ordinary, if highly intelligent, kid that I am. So, I decided to think of my special power's person as Bulk.

I can't just call on Bulk whenever I want. He chooses when he's going to make an appearance. So, I find it best to think of us as separate people - almost.

14

Chapter 2

I tried to explain to my parents about Bulk. But it didn't go very well.

"Hey Dad, I have special powers, you know," I said to my Daddy, one day, as he was watching football on the TV. He glanced away from the football match for a second, and replied, "Awk, do you son. That's great. They'll really help you with your homework."

As if I need any help with my homework.

I tried again, "No, no, you don't understand, Dad. These are REAL special powers."
He didn't even bother looking away from the TV this time, "Well, would you make Liverpool score a couple of goals here. We're losing one nil."

It wasn't any better when I told my Mammy: "Hey Mammy, just to let you know that I have special powers."
"Yes, your daddy was telling me, darling. But don't you worry about Liverpool losing today, sure it was only a football match, anyway," she said.
That's when I gave up trying to explain to the parents.

Abigail and I have four grandparents. Nanny and Dadda Carmichael, and Nanny and Dadda Abbot. We often have sleep-overs at each of their houses. And sometimes us and our parents go on holidays with them. They are all very good to Abigail and me.

Even Grumpy Dadda. Which is what I sometimes call Dadda Abbot, who can be a bit of a grump at times. But he and I get along fine. He's not always a grump, and when he is it's only because he's really old.

I sometimes babysit Grumpy Dadda. Keeping him company when Nanny Abbot has to stay overnight with the old people that she looks after. So, I suppose, just like her in a way, I'm a carer of old people too. Well, of one old person, anyway.
My sister and I go to a special school in Northern Ireland. No, not that kind of special school. It's called an integrated school, where kids of every religion and skin colour are educated together.

Our school is great. They sometimes teach us about history, which I love. Even though it makes me very angry at times.

Last year, during Black History Month, our teacher was telling us about a woman in America called Rosa Parks, who was made to give up her seat on a bus to a white person. Rosa was told to sit at the back of the bus. Just because she was Black. I couldn't believe this had really happened. But my teacher told me it was a true story. I was so angry about it. If Bulk had been there in those days, he would have made the driver sit at the back of the bus and allowed Rosa to drive it.

I told Grumpy Dadda the story about Rosa Parks, and how angry it had made me. "Oh yes, son," he said, "I remember that well. It was terrible."

He told me lots of other stories he remembered about that time in America. It's really good to have a very old Dadda for things like this. Even if he is a bit grumpy at times.

For a long time, Bulk didn't need to appear very often in my life. In fact, everyone around me was so nice, there was no need for him. At times I almost forgot that he existed.
But all of that changed when a kid called Ron joined our school.
Ron is the same age as me, so he joined my class. He seemed very friendly to everyone at the start. But after a while he started being cheeky with the teachers.

When Mrs Eglington would say to him, "Good morning, Ronald." He would reply, "Good morning, Mrs Eggshell." And to Mr Biggerstaff, he would ask, "Please sir, Mr Biggerstick, may I go to the bathroom?"
Even after the teachers had reminded him lots of times of their real names, he kept doing it. So they sent for his parents.
He stopped being cheeky to the teachers after that. But began to make fun of the other pupils instead.

He told Alice that her glasses made her look like a goldfish; kept asking Rosy if her ponytail meant that she was a horse; and started calling Patrick cow-pats. Eventually he had nicknames for everyone, including me. I was Smarty-Pants Wally because I got so many questions right in class.

Bulk didn't appear During all this time either. He didn't need to. It was only kids' stuff. And we all soon got used to the nicknames, so they didn't really bother anyone. Well, not until Ron took it too far, and was told what everyone was calling him behind his back.

One day he kept asking Liam, who he called Sore-Foot, why with a name like his he wasn't limping. Liam finally lost his temper, glared at him, and said, "I'd rather be called Sore-Foot than Rotten Ron."
Everyone started laughing, and saying things like, "Hey, Rotten Ron, why are you so nasty to everyone?"
Ron went very red and walked away.

After that, he never called anyone by a nickname again. But that doesn't mean he stopped picking on people. Oh no. He got worse. If a girl was sitting in front of him in class, when the teacher wasn't looking, he would pull her hair. If it was a boy, he would nip him or punch him in the back.

One day, he began sticking a sharp pencil into Henry's back. Which was very dangerous. That's when Bulk took over. My finger pointed at Ron, and my voice whispered, "Stop that, right now."

He didn't stop trying to poke Henry right away. His hand holding the pencil seemed to stick in mid-air for a few seconds, as if it was trying hard to push towards Henry before it went back down to his desk.

Ron glared across at me, "So you have Special Powers, too," he said, "You're now my enemy. Let's see who is the strongest."

I was shocked. It seemed that here was another kid with Special Powers. A bad kid.

When I got home from school that day, and thought about my fall-out with Ron, I kept wondering if he really had Special Powers. After all, what's the chances of two kids from the same school – two kids from the same class - having such powers?
But, then again, how did he know that I had Special Powers? And how was he able to almost stop Bulk from stopping him poking Henry with the pencil?
I was soon to find out for sure about Ron.

One day soon after Ron had told me I was his enemy, he called me over to him in the playground. "Hi Walter, would you like to play?" he asked me. I was shocked, but happy that he wanted to make friends.

But when I got close to him, he punched me right in the face and I fell to the ground. "You silly wee boy," he snarled, "did you really think I wanted to be friends with you?"

I glanced up at him from the ground, and to my surprise he was dressed in a Power Boy outfit. A very scary one. And his face was all twisted with anger.

Now I knew for sure that Ron had special powers. Bad ones.

It was then that Bulk took over. I felt an awful lot of energy go through my body, and I sprang to my feet. Now Rotten Ron and Bulk were facing one another again.

Bulk stretched out both of his arms, pointed them at Rotten Ron, and said in a very loud, thundery voice. "Stop it now, Rotten Ron."

Ron thundered back at Bulk, "No, you wimp, I'm going to punch you on the nose again. I've been practising my strength, and I am going to defeat you." But his voice was shaking a bit, and he looked a wee bit scared.

He had indeed been building up his strength. For it took all of Bulk's energy to hold him off. He was soon starting to feel totally exhausted.

Then, just as Bulk began to think that he would be defeated, Rotten Ron sank to the ground and

squeaked at Bulk, "I give up. But only for now. I will be back to get you, Bulk."
And with that, his costume disappeared, and he suddenly looked like an ordinary little boy again.

Even more amazing, during the fight I had noticed for the first time that Bulk was wearing a Special Boy costume. And it too disappeared when Rotten Ron gave up.

And even MORE amazing than that, lots of the other pupils had gathered around me and Ron during the big fight, but none of them appeared to have seen the costumes.

"What happened?" and "What was all that about?", they asked me. But not one of them mentioned our Special Boy costumes. "Oh, just another argument between Ron and me," is all I told them.

But I knew that this was just the start.

Rotten Ron would be back. And I had to learn how to help Bulk build up his strength, ready for the battles ahead. Perhaps I can contact a friendly alien to help Bulk.

Whatever happens, Rotten Ron must not be allowed to win.

(You'll find out all about it in my next book.)

Printed in Great Britain
by Amazon